D0686041

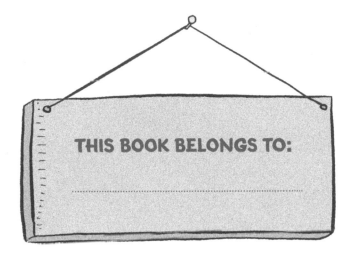

THIS BOOK BELONGS TO:

_____

CAMPING ACTIVITY BOOK *for Kids*

⇒35⇐ Fun Projects for Your Next Outdoor Adventure

AMELIA MAYER

Illustrated by Adam Larkum

ROCKRIDGE
PRESS

Copyright © 2021 by Rockridge Press, Emeryville, California

No part of this publication may be reproduced, stored in a retrieval system, or transmitted in any form or by any means, electronic, mechanical, photocopying, recording, scanning, or otherwise, except as permitted under Sections 107 or 108 of the 1976 United States Copyright Act, without the prior written permission of the Publisher. Requests to the Publisher for permission should be addressed to the Permissions Department, Rockridge Press, 6005 Shellmound Street, Suite 175, Emeryville, CA 94608.

Limit of Liability/Disclaimer of Warranty: The Publisher and the author make no representations or warranties with respect to the accuracy or completeness of the contents of this work and specifically disclaim all warranties, including without limitation warranties of fitness for a particular purpose. No warranty may be created or extended by sales or promotional materials. The advice and strategies contained herein may not be suitable for every situation. This work is sold with the understanding that the Publisher is not engaged in rendering medical, legal, or other professional advice or services. If professional assistance is required, the services of a competent professional person should be sought. Neither the Publisher nor the author shall be liable for damages arising herefrom. The fact that an individual, organization, or website is referred to in this work as a citation and/or potential source of further information does not mean that the author or the Publisher endorses the information the individual, organization, or website may provide or recommendations they/it may make. Further, readers should be aware that websites listed in this work may have changed or disappeared between when this work was written and when it is read.

For general information on our other products and services or to obtain technical support, please contact our Customer Care Department within the United States at (866) 744-2665, or outside the United States at (510) 253-0500.

Rockridge Press publishes its books in a variety of electronic and print formats. Some content that appears in print may not be available in electronic books, and vice versa.

TRADEMARKS: Rockridge Press and the Rockridge Press logo are trademarks or registered trademarks of Callisto Media Inc. and/or its affiliates, in the United States and other countries, and may not be used without written permission. All other trademarks are the property of their respective owners. Rockridge Press is not associated with any product or vendor mentioned in this book.

Interior and Cover Designer: Tricia Jang
Art Producer: Tom Hood
Editor: Elizabeth Baird
Production Editor: Matt Burnett
Production Manager: Michael Kay

Illustrations © Adam Larkum, 2021

ISBN: Print 978-1-64876-209-3 | eBook 978-1-64876-210-9
R0

This book is for my husband
and our five children, the
ultimate adventure buddies and
the loves of my life. I'm so
blessed by Team Mayer.

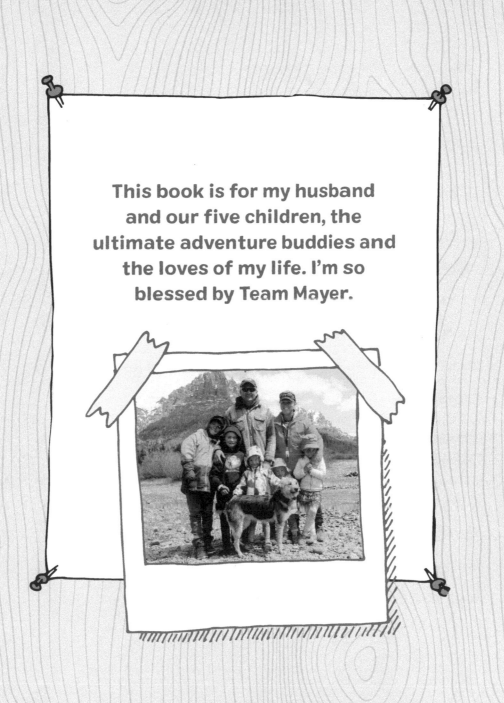

CONTENTS

A NOTE TO PARENTS

As a mom of five children (ages 3 to 11), finding a bit of sanity can be hard. But I have always found peace in the outdoors. My husband and I worked hard to make an outdoor life for our kids "normal." It's where we go to re-center and where we find family cohesiveness.

Spending time in the outdoors is a necessity for every kid. Children with a connection to nature build confidence and self-assurance; they learn to find their own paths as they grow and mature.

The 35 activities in this book help kids build the tools they need to navigate life's rough waters. Each activity is organized so that one skill builds upon the next. Some children will need a helping hand to complete the skill. Once they've colored in all of their badges and signed the Outdoors Oath (see page xii), they can keep this book handy in their backpack.

Sometimes getting out the door is the hardest part. Consider this book a little nudge, a way to bring the outdoors to your kids and have fun doing it.

A CHECKLIST FOR PARENTS

Camping references in this book usually mean "car camping." You can drive your car directly to the campsite, where you'll have easy access to the car for gear and campsite amenities.

Backpacking means carrying everything you need on your person. (Children should carry no more than 15–20 percent of their body weight.) To ensure a fun and successful family backpacking trip, plan hikes that are less than two miles in length and with a modest elevation gain. To limit weight, be sure to bring only what you need.

Here's a basic gear list to help get your kids excited and prepared for a trip in the great outdoors. Of course, it's not exhaustive, but it will get you started with the most important stuff:

☐ Backpack
☐ Bedroll or sleeping pad
☐ Camp chair
☐ Clothing layers for hot and cold weather, including hat and gloves
☐ Headlamp (with batteries) and a battery-operated light for the tent
☐ Hiking shoes or boots and hiking socks
☐ Pillow (either a camp pillow or one from home)
☐ Sleeping bag
☐ Tent
☐ Water bottle and water filter (if no access to potable water)

1. Back pack
2. Bandana
3. Camp chair
4. Clothing layers
5. Headlamp
6. Hiking boots
7. Small Pillow
8. Sleeping bag & pad
9. Tent
10. Water bottle

A NOTE ON THE ACTIVITIES IN THIS BOOK

While kids can do many of the activities in this book on their own, they are usually more fun with a friend or trusted adult. The following activities require parental help (look for the icon on those pages):

Pitch a Tent (page 2)

Build a Fire (page 3)

Build a Shelter (page 5)

S'more for Me! (page 8)

Make a Compass (page 14)

Walking Tall (page 19)

Treasure Hunt (page 23)

Magnifying Magic (page 26)

Counting Constellations (page 50)

Water Warrior (page 59)

Make a Finding Flag (page 60)

The Whys and Wheres of Camping

Camping is not easy for everyone. Some families live in an urban area far from nature; transportation to more rural locations can be hard to come by. Mobility challenges can make camping a burden, while others can't afford the gear, campground fees, or vacation time off to go. But camping *is* for everyone—it just might take extra effort to get there.

The Resources section (page 68) lists a few of the many incredible programs and foundations that believe in getting kids into nature. These programs work hard to help you make that happen. They are life-changing for many families and could be for yours. Even if you can't get outdoors, many of the activities can be practiced almost anywhere or can be modified for an urban environment.

WELCOME, OUTDOOR ADVENTURER!

Hi, kids! Welcome to your outdoor adventure! Are you ready to learn some really important skills and have fun in the outdoors? This book will teach you everything you need to know to enjoy being a good **steward**, or caretaker, of the wilderness. Once you've completed all the activities and earned and colored in your badges, you'll become an official **Outdoor Adventurer**. That's a big deal and a big responsibility—one you should be very proud of!

MY OUTDOORS OATH

Read the Outdoors Oath. Then sign your name to make it official.

I promise to teach others what I learn and to protect nature so that everyone can enjoy it for years to come. I will do my best to be prepared, take care of the Earth, stay safe, and Leave No Trace when I am out in the wilderness.

Signed: _____

PACK THE BARE NECESSITIES

Outdoor Adventurers are well prepared to keep everyone safe and having fun. Keep these bare necessities in your adventure pack so that you're always ready to go.

- ☐ First-aid kit
- ☐ Hand sanitizer
- ☐ Headlamp and/or flashlight
- ☐ Jacket or extra layer of clothing
- ☐ Map and compass
- ☐ Raincoat and/or survival blanket
- ☐ Rope or twine
- ☐ Signal mirror
- ☐ Snacks
- ☐ Sunscreen, hat, and bandana
- ☐ This book and a pen or pencil
- ☐ Toilet paper (in a small zip-top bag)
- ☐ Water bottle
- ☐ Whistle

CHAPTER ONE

HELLO, CAMPSITE!

Setting up your very own campsite is the perfect way to settle in for a night outdoors. While every campsite looks a little different, there are some important parts to learn to keep you safe and having fun.

In this chapter, you'll learn the following skills:

- ☐ **How to pitch a tent**
- ☐ **How to build a fire**
- ☐ **How to build a shelter**
- ☐ **Knot-tying basics**
- ☐ **How to make a lantern**
- ☐ **Campfire activities**

PITCH A TENT

Getting a good night of rest starts with a comfortable place to sleep. And that means you need to set up your tent in the best location.

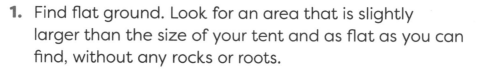

1. Find flat ground. Look for an area that is slightly larger than the size of your tent and as flat as you can find, without any rocks or roots.

2. Avoid putting your tent under any dead trees or limbs, in case they fall down. Look for a place with healthy trees to provide shade.

3. Lay out your tent. Use tent stakes to ground the corners of your tent. Finally, attach the tent poles to the tent.

4. Don't forget your rain fly. This is a cover that goes over your tent and keeps it dry if it rains. If your tent doesn't have a rain fly, tie a tarp above your tent for added shelter. Use a bowline knot (see the activity on page 6) to tie it down.

Camping at Home

Before you ever arrive at the campsite, it's a good idea to practice pitching your tent in your living room or in a backyard with an adult. All tents are different, and they do take a little practice. When you get to the campsite, challenge yourself to set up the tent on your own.

NOW YOU KNOW!

Now you know how to find a good location and pitch your tent. That's one skill down, six to go to earn your campsite badge!

BUILD A FIRE

No campsite is complete without a fire. Have an adult help you with this activity. It's best to build your fire in a designated fire ring or fire pit. However, if there is not one available, you can make your own using rocks. The most important thing is to never leave a fire alone.

1. If there isn't a fire ring at your campsite, build one with a ring of rocks. Clear the area around the fire ring of plants and grass.

2. Gather dry **tinder** (grasses, leaves, and shredded bark), **kindling** (small twigs and sticks smaller than your forearm), and **firewood** (larger logs).

3. Form an upright triangle in the ring (like a teepee) with the logs. Leave space in the middle to lay the tinder and kindling and allow oxygen to get through.

4. In the space you made in the middle of the teepee, carefully lay the tinder and then loosely place the kindling.

5. Ask your adult to carefully light the tinder with a match or lighter. Blow gently on the small flames. This will "catch" the kindling and then light the firewood.

CONTINUES →

6. Always stay close by your fire. When you're done, put the fire completely out by dumping cold water on it. Campfires should be cold to the touch before they're safe to leave.

Light It Up

Building a fire is not only fun—it's a great way to cook your food or keep warm. Only build a fire when an adult is with you and you have permission to do so. Check the campsite regulations before you start. A good fire is a safe fire.

NOW YOU KNOW!

Now you know how to build a fire, and you know how and where to pitch a tent. Keep going!

BUILD A SHELTER

Building a shelter while camping is a fun way to make your own little home wherever you are. You can do this anytime you're in the woods.

1. Gather some materials around you to use. Are there sticks or logs? Leaves or grasses? You can build a shelter with almost anything you can find. Try to find a large branch to use as the base of your shelter (this should come from the ground—never harm a tree or bush by ripping off its branches).

2. Lean the end of the big branch against a large tree (one with a "Y" shape in the trunk is best). Ask an adult to help with this part to make sure the branch won't move.

3. To make the sides, lean other large sticks against the big branch to make a lean-to.

4. Fill in the gaps with leaves and grasses.

Try It Indoors

It's fun to make a fort at home, too. Find a clear spot in your bedroom or living room. Spread three or four blankets over a table, tie them between a couch and a chair, or even hang them from a bunk bed.

KNOTS TO KNOW

Knowing how to tie a bowline knot in rope will help you with many camping activities. The bowline knot is sturdy and easy to untie.

1. Start with the rope in a "U" position, with one end longer. Form a loop in the long end of the line. This is called a "rabbit hole."

2. Pass the working end (the shorter end, or the "rabbit") of the line under and through the loop, then around and behind the long end of the rope ("the tree").

3. Pass the "rabbit" back down through the original loop (that's the "rabbit hole"), while keeping the shape of the second loop.

4. Once the "rabbit" is back down its hole, pull the long end ("the tree") up to tighten the bowline.

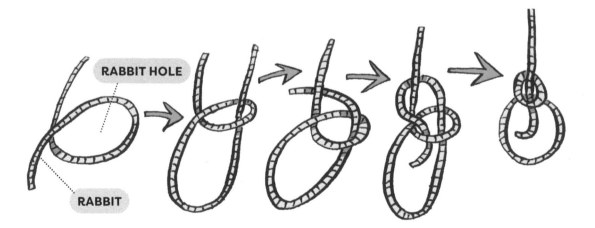

The Most Useful Knot in the World

The bowline knot is extremely useful, especially for camping. Here's what you can do with it:

- Tie a hammock to a tree.
- Hang your food high on a tree branch so it is far away from critters.
- Secure a pet while you get the campsite ready.
- Hang a tarp to use as a rain fly or shelter.
- Tie two ropes together.

NOW YOU KNOW!

Now you're a knot wizard! The bowline knot is a good first knot to know. Challenge yourself to learn other important camping knots.

S'MORE FOR ME!

S'mores are a classic camping dessert and a delicious way to end a fun day outdoors. Here's how to make the best s'mores.

1. Build a fire (see page 3). Let the fire burn down until only hot coals are left.

2. Put one marshmallow onto the clean, pointed end of a long, thin stick. (Ask an adult to help you carve the pointy end.)

3. Carefully hold the stick a little above the coals to roast the marshmallow. Turn the stick so that all sides of the marshmallow cook to a golden brown. Be careful not to let the marshmallow touch the coals or catch fire. If it does, quickly blow it out.

4. Once it's browned, remove the marshmallow from the fire. Place some chocolate on a graham cracker and carefully put your hot marshmallow on top. Sandwich with a second graham cracker and pull the marshmallow off the stick. Eat up!

More S'mores

There are so many yummy ways to make s'mores. Try some of these ingredients to make different s'mores combos. Anything goes!

The Classic: chocolate + marshmallow + graham crackers

Elvis: chocolate + marshmallow + banana + peanut butter + graham crackers

Fruity: dark chocolate + strawberry slice + marshmallow + graham crackers

Gooey: chocolate bar with caramel filling + marshmallow + graham crackers

Oreo: chocolate + marshmallow + Oreos

Peanut Butter Time: Reese's Peanut Butter Cup + marshmallow + graham crackers

Sweet and Salty: caramel + marshmallow + saltine crackers

Tropical: white chocolate + shredded coconut + dried pineapple slice + marshmallow + graham crackers

NOW YOU KNOW!

Now you know some basic campfire cooking. Don't forget to pack some fun ingredients for your next trip to take your s'mores to the next level.

SHINE A LIGHT

Learn how to make a really cool campsite lantern that you can use in your tent, on a camping table, or anywhere you need light.

WHAT YOU'LL NEED:

☐ Headlamp

☐ Plastic milk jug (empty)

☐ Carabiner (to hang it)

☐ Markers (optional)

1. Stretch the band of the headlamp around the empty milk jug so that the light will shine inward into the jug. If the headlamp feels loose, tighten the band or wrap it around the jug twice.

2. Grab the carabiner and clip it onto the jug handle.

3. If you want, use your markers to decorate the outside of the jug.

4. Turn on the headlamp. Now you have a lantern to hang inside your tent.

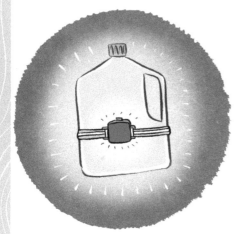

Shadow Show

It can be fun to decorate your lantern with markers and make it all your own. When it's hung, the designs on your lantern will cast cool shadow shapes on the walls of your tent. Write your name, draw animals or people—anything goes!

TELL A CAMPFIRE STORY

At the end of the night, when your tent is pitched and you've started a fire, gather everyone around the campsite and tell your very own campfire story. Use your own words to fill in the blanks below. Here's a hint: a noun is a person, place, or thing; verbs are action words (like run and jump); plural means "more than one" ("dogs" is the plural of "dog"). Have fun with it!

I am so excited! We are going camping and I am bringing

my _____, my _____, and my
      noun   noun

friend _____. I can't wait to set up my _____,
    name of a person   noun

make a _____, and _____ with my
        noun   verb

friend. For dinner we are going to eat _____ and
                              plural noun

roast _____ for dessert. Tomorrow we are going to
      plural noun

_____ in the woods. I hope we don't run into
    verb

any _____!
   plural noun

You've learned all the skills needed for your campsite badge. You know how to pitch a tent, build a fire, construct a shelter, and tie knots, and you learned some fun things to do while camping. **Color the badge!**

CHAPTER TWO

HIT THE TRAIL

Now that you've set up your campsite, it's time to hit the trail and explore. You'll need to learn navigational skills, like how to use a map and a compass, what trail markers are, and how to tell directions on a map. Once you learn these skills, you can lead your own hike.

In this chapter, you'll learn the following skills:

☐ **How to create a compass**

☐ **How to navigate**

☐ **How to make a walking stick**

☐ **How to draw your own map**

☐ **How to read trail signs**

MAKE A COMPASS

When you're exploring in the woods, how do you know which way to go? By using a compass, of course. A compass is one of the most important tools for an outdoor adventurer. It shows you where the directions north, south, east, and west are. Let's make one!

WHAT YOU'LL NEED:

☐ Strong magnet (science magnets are available online, but even a strong fridge magnet works)

☐ Large sewing needle (3 inches long)

☐ A cork

☐ Knife to cut cork

☐ Large (8-inch diameter) unbreakable bowl (plastic works best)

☐ Water

☐ 4 small pieces of paper labeled N, S, E, and W

1. Magnetize the needle by rubbing the magnet across one side of the needle from top to bottom. Do this about 60 times (or for 1 minute).

2. Now, flip the needle and the magnet over to the other side and rub the magnet from the bottom to the top of the needle 60 times (or for 1 minute).

3. Cut the cork with a knife so it is about ½ inch thick, and carefully stick the needle through the middle of the cork. (This is a good job for an adult.)

4. Fill the bowl with 2 inches of water and float the cork in the water. The needle will point north.

5. Tape the "N" paper (for north) on the edge of the bowl where the needle is pointing north. Look at the drawing on the next page to see where to add the S (south), E (east), and W (west) papers on the bowl.

Which North Is North?

The magnet of a compass points to **magnetic north**, which is actually a little different than **true north**, and that can get really confusing, really fast. Unlike true north, magnetic north is constantly moving. It moves about 10 kilometers per year due to changes in Earth's magnetic field. There's a word called "declination" that explains how "off" your compass will be from true north depending on where you are in the world. For now, it's most important to know that because the magnetic North Pole is a bit different from the true North Pole, a compass doesn't point exactly north, but it's pretty close.

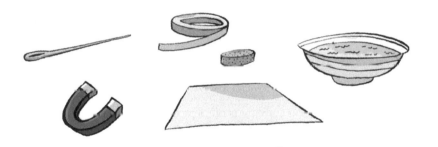

WHICH WAY?

Maps are a fun way to learn about where you are and where you are going. In this activity, you will learn how to read a map.

1. Study a map of a trail, city, or town. Every map has the same main elements.

2. Look for the "compass rose." It's a star-shaped symbol with an N at the top. Each letter on the compass—N (north), E (east), S (south), and W (west)— stands for one of the four directions on the compass rose. Here's an easy way to remember them: out loud, say "**N**ever **E**at **S**hredded **W**heat" (because it rhymes and it's fun to say).

3. Find the legend—a box of information that contains symbols and their connected meanings. These symbols are often drawn on the map to identify important locations or bits of information. For example, a tent symbol is a place where you can camp.

4. Use the legend to identify and match up symbols on the map.

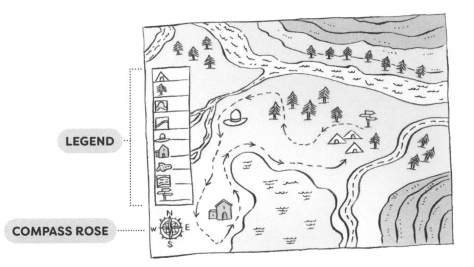

LEGEND

COMPASS ROSE

Using a Map and Compass Together

A compass is cool, and a map is great, but using them together is how you navigate. Lay your map down on a flat surface. Then, set your compass down on your map so that the "north" of the map's compass rose points in the same direction as the homemade compass's "north." Now you know which way is magnetic north. Your map might also have a "declination calculator" if you want to find true north—ask an adult for help to figure this out!

NOW YOU KNOW!

Now you know how to navigate using a map and a compass. With these skills, you can figure out which way you're going and how to get there. The next activity will help you get there even more easily.

MAKE A MAP

Now it's time to make your very own map and test it out with family and friends.

WHAT YOU'LL NEED:

☐ Paper

☐ Pencil

☐ Colored pencils or crayons

1. First, think of what you want your map to show, like where your tent is, or how to get around your neighborhood. Make a list of the items to include on your map: buildings, trees, rivers, etc.

2. On your map, identify north, south, east, and west using your compass, and draw on a compass rose.

3. Draw symbols on your map to represent the list of places you identified in step 1. This includes anything you can see that will help others understand your map.

4. Add a map legend that explains the symbols. A tent could mean your campsite, or a fish could mean there's a river with good fishing.

Follow That Trail!

Now it's the fun part. Grab a buddy (and an adult) and use your new map to get to where you need to go. Ask your buddy to read your map. Can they tell how to get to one of the places you labeled?

WALKING TALL

Making a walking stick is a fun activity to do before you go on a hike. Walking sticks can help you keep your balance on the trail, cross creeks, and push uphill as you explore.

WHAT YOU'LL NEED:

☐ Large, straight stick

☐ Knife (for carving)

☐ Sandpaper (bring from home)

1. Find a large sturdy stick that's as tall as your shoulders.

2. With the help of an adult, use the knife to strip the bark from the stick and remove any small twigs. Shave off any parts of the stick that are poking out.

3. Use the sandpaper to smooth the surface so that it is easy to hold.

4. Test it out. Walk around with your stick. Does it feel smooth? Is it tall enough? Can it help you out on the trail?

For Your Journey

Make your walking stick even more special by turning it into a Journey Stick. On your first hike with your new walking stick, look for small items on the ground, such as leaves or flowers. When you get home, tie your found treasures onto your stick as a souvenir from your hike. You can also paint your stick or add anything else fun that makes it special and yours.

IT'S A SIGN!

When hiking on a trail, different signs tell you which way to go—and whether you're still on the right trail. Some signs are obvious, but others are harder to read. Here are the top three signs and how to read them.

Trail Sign: Look for a wooden or metal sign along the trail that lists the destination (like "Taggert Lake") or the name of the trail. Some signs tell which direction to go and how many miles it is to get there. You'll see trail signs at trail **junctions**, places where one or more trails connect. They'll help you know which way to turn.

Trail Blaze: Trail blazes are colored shapes (like a rectangle) painted high on the trunks of trees that mark the path. Sometimes they are small, colored pieces of metal that are nailed to the tree. If you're hiking a "blue-blazed" trail, look for trees with blue paint or blue metal pieces on them.

Cairn: Cairns (also called trail ducks) are piles of small, stacked rocks. They are used to mark trails where there may not be many trees or where the ground is too hard to post a trail sign. Cairns can usually only point a hiker in one direction: straight ahead.

How to Read Trail Blazes

Here are some common symbols you might see on a trail.

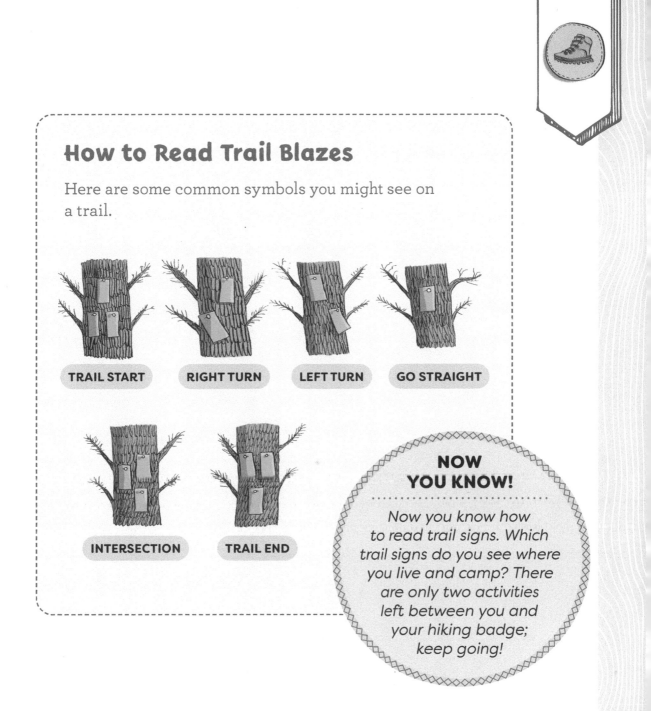

TRAIL START

RIGHT TURN

LEFT TURN

GO STRAIGHT

INTERSECTION

TRAIL END

NOW YOU KNOW!

Now you know how to read trail signs. Which trail signs do you see where you live and camp? There are only two activities left between you and your hiking badge; keep going!

CAMPGROUND MAZE

Look at all those skills you learned. Now test your outdoor adventure skills with this campground maze. Can you follow the maze to find where "x" marks the spot?

TREASURE HUNT

Creating your own treasure hunt is a super fun way to test your navigational skills. Pull out your compass for this game and practice the four cardinal directions: north, south, east, and west.

WHAT YOU'LL NEED:

☐ A small treasure to hide

☐ Compass

☐ Paper

☐ Pen or pencil

1. Hide a small treasure somewhere near the campsite. This could be an action figure, a piece of candy, a ball, etc.

2. Choose your starting point. Use your compass to figure out how many steps north, south, east, or west there are from your starting point to the treasure.

3. Write the number of steps in each direction, in order, that it will take to get to the treasure from the starting point. For example: five steps north, then three steps west, and so on.

4. Give the directions to a friend and see if they can find the hidden treasure.

Outstanding! You've created a compass and map, learned how to read a map, made your own special walking stick, learned to recognize and read trail signs, and tested your skills with a treasure hunt. That means you've earned your hiking badge! **Color the badge!**

CHAPTER THREE

LET'S GO WILD

In this chapter, you'll learn to identify wild plants and trees as you hike and camp. You'll also learn how to find and identify animal tracks, which is a super fun way to figure out which creatures are sharing your space while you're in the great outdoors.

In this chapter, you'll learn the following skills:

☐ **How to make your own magnifying glass**

☐ **How to identify insects**

☐ **How to identify the different parts of leaves and flowers**

☐ **How to identify animal tracks and scat**

☐ **How to tell the age of a tree**

MAGNIFYING MAGIC

A magnifying glass is one of the best tools to study the natural world around you. Learn to make your very own magnifying glass that you can use for the activities in this chapter. This project is best done at home before you get to the campsite.

WHAT YOU'LL NEED:

- ☐ Ruler

- ☐ 2-liter soda bottle (empty)

- ☐ Permanent marker

- ☐ Scissors

- ☐ Hot glue gun

- ☐ Water

- ☐ Zip ties (at least 3)

- ☐ Small stick (about ½ inch thick and 4 inches long)

1. Draw two 3-inch circles on the curved top of the soda bottle (near the spout) with the marker.

2. With scissors, carefully cut out the circles you drew.

3. Now, ask an adult to glue the two circles together with the glue gun, leaving an opening unglued. The circles should make a "pocket" with a 1-inch open space.

4. Once the glue dries, carefully fill the pocket with tap water. Ask your adult helper to glue the pocket opening closed, and then let it dry.

5. Wrap a zip tie around the glued circles and tighten it. Attach the stick to the tail of the zip tie using at least two more zip ties. This creates a handle.

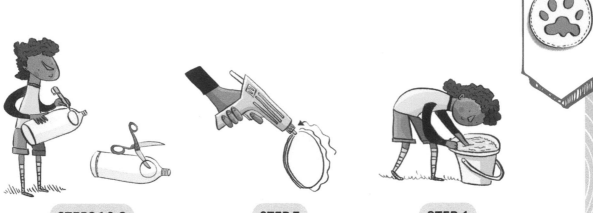

STEPS 1 & 2   **STEP 3**   **STEP 4**

STEP 5

Bigger in a Hurry

Here's a quicker way to make a magnifying glass that's just as good. Cut a circle (3 to 4 inches wide) out of a large soda bottle near the lid. Use the circle as the "dish" of the magnifying glass and add some water to it. The round part of the plastic helps magnify images. Now you can look at nature up close.

NOW YOU KNOW!

Now you know how to make your own magnifying glass. Next, you'll practice using your magnifying glass to discover tiny details about bugs, butterflies, flowers, and more.

BUG OUT

It's time to put you magnifying glass to the test. Take an up-close look at insects. Bugs have lots of interesting body parts that you can only see up close.

1. Look on flowers, tree branches, and the ground to find a safe, harmless insect (see "Safety First," page 29).

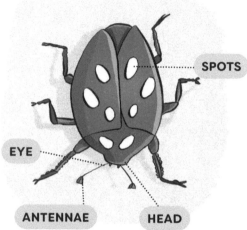

2. Look closely at your insect with your magnifying glass. Insects have six legs. Can you see and count them all?

3. Now, use your magnifying glass to look at the head of your insect. Most insects have two antennae, used to smell. Can you find them?

4. Most insects have four wings, but some only have two. How many pairs of wings can you count on your insect?

5. Draw your insect in the space below:

Safety First

Not all insects are safe to study up close. Some bugs to avoid include bees and wasps (as well as their nests). Bees and wasps don't like to be bothered—they might sting you.

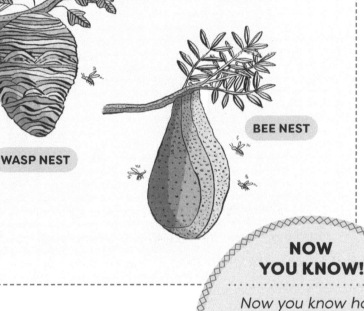

WASP NEST

BEE NEST

NOW YOU KNOW!

Now you know how to examine an insect. How many types of bugs can you discover? Next you'll look closely at flowers and other plants.

FLOWER POWER

Flowers can be found almost anywhere you go camping, depending on the season, of course. In this activity, find a flower on the ground so that you can learn all its different parts. Don't pick it! Instead, study it where it grows.

Petals: Petals are usually the most colorful part of a flower and what we look for first. How many petals can you count on your flower?

Leaves: All flowers have leaves. Leaves are how flowers use energy from the sun to make food for the flower. How many leaves are on your flower? Do they all look the same or are some leaves smaller?

Stem: The stem of a flower connects it to the ground so that it can stay tall. Is your flower's stem long or short?

Pistil: In the center of the flower is the pistil. The pistil includes a flower's pollen and lets the flower **reproduce**, or make more flowers. Look carefully. What do you see?

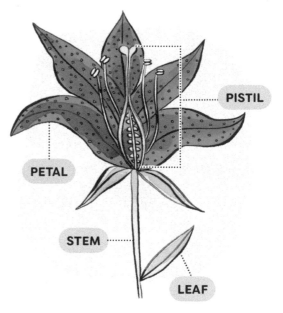

PISTIL

PETAL

STEM

LEAF

A Scent-Filled Scrapbook

One way to keep a flower for a long time is to press and dry it.

1. Find a small flower on the ground, something that has already dropped from a tree or bush.
2. Carefully fold the flower in a paper towel and put it inside a heavy book. Close the book and stack some more books on top of it to help flatten, or press, the flower.
3. The flower should dry out in 2 to 3 weeks.
4. Carefully glue your pressed and dried flower to a piece of paper so that you can always look at it.

NOW YOU KNOW!

Now you know how to identify the different parts of a flower. Try learning names of different flowers. Save a flower from each place you visit (if it's okay to pick them) to remember each place.

FLORA FUN

Leaves have many amazing parts that you may miss unless you look carefully. Find some leaves on the ground (after checking "Safety First" on page 33) and see if you can identify these parts using your magnifying glass.

Petiole: The petiole is the stem of a leaf where the leaf attaches to a tree. The petiole of a leaf is flexible so that it can move in the wind and not break.

Blade: The blade is the whole flat part of a leaf. It includes the apex, the veins, and the midrib.

Apex: The tip of a leaf is called its apex. (The word apex means "pointed end.") Is the apex of your leaf pointy or more rounded?

Veins: Veins are a leaf's highways. They transport water to the leaf and carry food back to the plant.

Midrib: The midrib is the main vein of the leaf. It runs from the petiole to the apex. It is the "highway" that gives the leaf its structure.

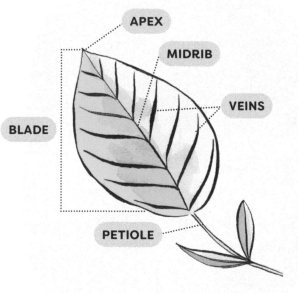

Safety First

When studying leaves, it's natural to want to touch them. But some leaves are not safe to touch. Poison oak and poison ivy can give you an itchy rash that is no fun at all. How can you tell a good leaf from an itchy one? Poison oak and poison ivy have leaves in groups of three. So, remember the saying: "Leaves of three, let it be!"

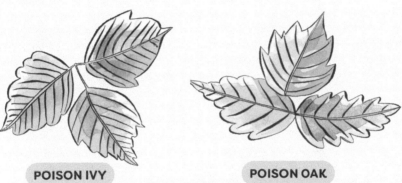

POISON IVY

POISON OAK

NOW YOU KNOW!

Now you know how to identify the different parts of a leaf. When you explore outdoors, look carefully at all of the leaves and plants around you. Show someone you love the different parts of your leaf. Next, you'll learn how to spot signs that animals have been in an area.

ANIMAL INSTINCTS

Animal tracks and scat (that's poop!) can tell you which animals are around you. They take an Outdoor Adventurer's careful observation to spot. Hint: Mud and snow make it easier to find animal tracks after a wet day.

1. When camping near water, look at the ground to see if you can spot any animal tracks.

2. How many sets of tracks are there? More tracks will make it easier to study and figure out what the animal was doing.

3. Which direction are they going? Look for claws in the tracks to help you figure this out.

4. What shape are they? Pointy, like a raccoon's? Hoof prints, like from a deer or a moose? Or do they look like tiny forks? A bird might have made those.

5. Look at the animal tracks on this page. Which animal do YOU think your tracks came from?

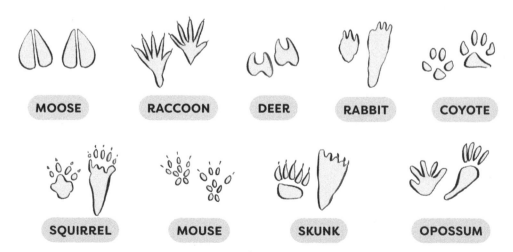

MOOSE   RACCOON   DEER   RABBIT   COYOTE

SQUIRREL   MOUSE   SKUNK   OPOSSUM

What Scat Is That?

Sometimes there aren't any tracks, but animals always leave a little something *else* behind. That's scat (or poop). Use the pictures below to help identify an animal by their scat.

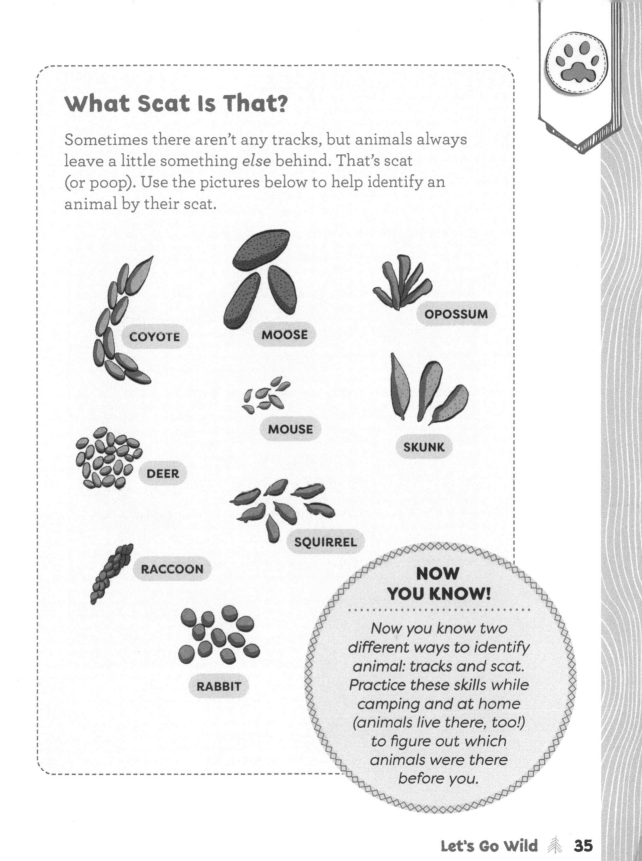

COYOTE

MOOSE

OPOSSUM

MOUSE

SKUNK

DEER

SQUIRREL

RACCOON

RABBIT

NOW YOU KNOW!

Now you know two different ways to identify animal: tracks and scat. Practice these skills while camping and at home (animals live there, too!) to figure out which animals were there before you.

COUNT THE RINGS

A tree can tell us lots of stories. One of those stories is how old it is. When a tree is cut down, we can count the rings on its stump to find out how old it was and how it lived.

1. Look carefully at the surface of a cut stump. You should see circles in the wood that grow in size from the center outward. These are called "growth rings."

2. Place your finger in the middle of the stump where the circles first begin. Now, count how many rings there are outward to the edge of the stump. Each ring equals one season, or one year.

3. Are some rings closer together while others are farther apart? If rings are close together, the tree didn't grow very much that year. Sometimes this happens during years when the winter is particularly long or there isn't enough rain. If the rings are wider apart, that means the tree grew a lot that year.

4. How many rings did you count? That's how old the tree was when it was cut down!

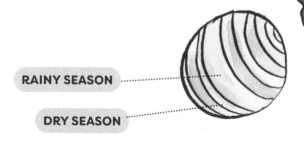

RAINY SEASON

DRY SEASON

FIRST YEAR GROWTH

Ancient Elders

Trees are very old. The first trees grew almost 400 million years ago. There are now about 3 *trillion* trees on Earth. Here's a short list of some special trees to look for.

Tallest – Giant sequoias (redwoods) are about 300 feet tall. The tallest tree on Earth is a redwood named "Hyperion" which is 379.7 feet tall.

Shortest – Dwarf willows are only 2 inches tall.

Oldest – One bristlecone pine in California is almost 5,000 years old.

Largest – The "General Sherman" giant sequoia is 52,000 cubic feet by volume.

Broadest – The "Great Banyan" tree in India has the broadest, or widest, crown, almost 600 feet across.

NOW YOU KNOW!

Now you know how a tree ages and grows. Do the next activity, and then you can color the badge you've earned.

I SPY

It's time to put your tree, animal, and insect knowledge to the test with this Outdoor Adventurer scavenger hunt. Go on a hike with your family and see how many you can spy. Cross out each item when you find it. You might not find them all in one hike!

Animal scat	A flower with more than four petals	A tree that you can wrap your arms around
A set of animal tracks	One leaf with a long petiole ("stem")	A tree stump with at least 10 rings
An insect with wings	A flower with yellow petals	A tree that's as tall as you are

Now you know how to make a magnifying glass and how to observe and identify insects, plants, and animals in the wild. Congratulations—you've earned your wildlife identification badge!
Color the badge!

CHAPTER FOUR

SKY-GAZING SUPERSTAR

Knowing how to read signs in the sky is an important part of being an Outdoor Adventurer. In this chapter, learn how to watch for different types of weather, how to tell time using the sun, and how to use the sun and stars to figure out which way to go.

In this chapter, you'll learn the following skills:

☐ **How to identify and interpret cloud shapes**

☐ **How to tell time using the sun**

☐ **How to tell when the sun will set**

☐ **How to find constellations in the night sky**

☐ **How to find true north**

CLOUDY WITH A CHANCE OF . . .

Clouds show us what kind of weather is happening in the sky and what weather is coming soon. See what clouds you can find in the sky and guess the weather that is coming.

Cumulus: These clouds look like fluffy white cotton balls and can resemble fun shapes. If you see cumulus (pronounced *kyoo-myuh-luhs*) clouds, then the weather is good.

Stratus: Stratus clouds stretch out in low, thin sheets across the sky. Stratus (pronounced *stray-tus*) clouds mean there might be a light drizzle.

Cirrus: These feathery clouds are so high up that they are made of ice particles. Cirrus (pronounced *see-ruhs*) clouds are often seen in a clear blue sky on fair-weather days. They mean that the weather might change soon.

Nimbus: These clouds are dark and puffy. Nimbus (pronounced *nim-buhs*) clouds usually mean rain or snow is coming—or is already falling!

Altostratus: These blue or gray clouds can cover the whole sky. Altostratus (pronounced *al-tow-stray-tuhs*) clouds usually mean that a storm is on its way.

Altocumulus: These gray or white clouds look like cotton balls all lined up in rows or clumps. If you see altocumulus (pronounced *al-tow-kyoo-myuh-luhs*) clouds in the morning, it could mean thunderstorms later in the day.

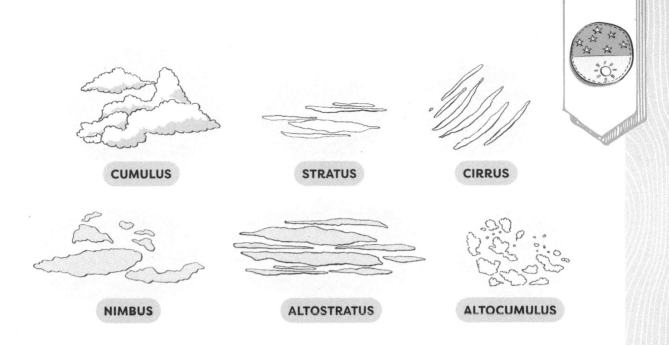

CUMULUS STRATUS CIRRUS

NIMBUS ALTOSTRATUS ALTOCUMULUS

Rain, Rain, Go Away!

Thunder and lightning can tell you whether an approaching storm is near or far. Light travels faster than sound, so you'll *see* lightning before you *hear* thunder. Here's how to tell how close a storm is:

1. When you see lightning, count the seconds ("1-Mississippi, 2-Mississippi," etc.) until you hear thunder.
2. Divide the number of seconds by 5.
3. For every 5 seconds, the storm is one mile away. For example, if you counted 10 seconds, divide the number 10 by 5 and you'll get the number 2. The storm is only 2 miles away!

If you see lightning or hear thunder while camping, get somewhere safe like the family car or somewhere protected and indoors.

TELLING TIME

How do you know what time it is? Today, you might look at a watch or a clock, but 2,500 years ago people used the sun to tell time. They did this by making a sundial—and you can make one, too. Plan to do this activity early on a sunny day, either at home or at a campsite.

WHAT YOU'LL NEED:

☐ Air-dry clay

☐ White paper plate

☐ Pencil

☐ Rock

☐ Markers

1. Roll the air-dry clay into a ball. Press the ball of clay into the middle of the paper plate.

2. Stick a pencil into the clay so it stands straight up. This is now your sundial.

3. Place your sundial on a flat surface, like the ground, and in a sunny place. Place a rock on it to keep it from being blown in the wind, if necessary.

4. Check your sundial starting at 9:00 a.m. Does your pencil cast a shadow? Trace the shadow line across the plate with a marker. Mark the end of the shadow with the number "9:00 a.m."

5. In one hour, check to see where the pencil's shadow falls. Mark the time as 10:00 a.m. Do this every hour, marking the hours until 3:00 p.m.

6. The next day, go out and check your sundial again. Can you tell what time it is just by looking at the shadow on the sundial?

NOW YOU KNOW!

Now you know how to tell time just by looking at a shadow. This will come in handy when you don't have a watch or a clock. But what if you need to know how much time is left before it gets dark? The next activity can help!

SETTING SUN

Did you know you can use your hand to see how soon the sun will set? This is an easy way to make sure you have enough time to set up camp before dark.

1. Stretch your arm out in front of you.

2. Bend your wrist so that your palm is facing you.

3. Hold your hand sideways so that your pointer finger is right under the sun and your pinky finger sits on the horizon (the line where the land and the sky appear to meet).

4. If you see more "sky" between your thumb and the sun, stack your other hand on top of your first hand.

5. Each finger equals 10 minutes before the sun sets. (For an adult hand, each finger equals 15 minutes). So, if you can fit one hand between the horizon and the sun, you'd better finish setting up camp in about 40 to 60 minutes.

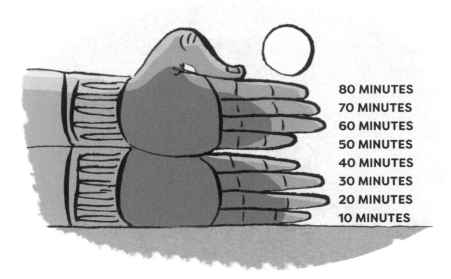

80 MINUTES
70 MINUTES
60 MINUTES
50 MINUTES
40 MINUTES
30 MINUTES
20 MINUTES
10 MINUTES

Super Sunsets

Have you ever wondered why sunsets can turn the sky different colors? As the sun begins to set below the horizon, its light must travel farther and farther through our atmosphere to reach us. This causes the light to "scatter." The more the light scatters, the less yellow color we can see. The colors that travel farthest are red and orange, and these are the colors we see the most just before the sun sets.

NOW YOU KNOW!

Now you know how to tell when the sun will set! Practice this skill with your hands and fingers each time you see a sunset. Keep going—you're nearly halfway to earning your sky-gazing badge.

SEE THE STARS

When you're camping outdoors, one of the best sights is an amazing night sky full of stars. In this activity, you will draw the constellations.

WHAT YOU'LL NEED:

☐ Black paper

☐ Pencil

☐ Pen (gold or silver)

1. Look up at the night sky and see if you can find any constellations—groups of visible stars that make up patterns or shapes. These could be the common ones like the Big Dipper (see page 50), or you might want to make up and name one yourself. Consider researching constellations before your camping trip to learn more.

2. Now draw the star pattern of a constellation you saw. On your black paper, draw dots with your pencil where your stars will be.

3. If you want, you can draw lines with your gold or silver pen between your stars to show how they are connected to make a constellation.

4. On each dot, carefully poke your pencil through the paper to make a small hole.

5. Shine a light through your paper or hold it up to the light in the morning to see your constellation shine.

STEP 1

STEP 2

STEPS 3 & 4

STEP 5

NOW YOU KNOW!

....

Now you know how to make a map of constellations you've seen in the night sky. See how many you can find. Next, you'll learn how to find one particular constellation.

COUNTING CONSTELLATIONS

The Big Dipper is part of the constellation called Ursa Major, and it's easy to find at night in the Northern Hemisphere because its bright stars stay above the horizon all night long. The stars in the Big Dipper form the shape of a pan with a handle, but, when they are combined with other stars, you can also see the shape of a bear. That's why the whole constellation is called Ursa Major, which means the Great Bear in Latin. Here is how to find it.

1. Once it is dark, use a compass, or spot Polaris (see page 52) to figure out which direction is north.

2. If you live in the Northern Hemisphere, look to the north on a clear night to find the Big Dipper. It will be in slightly different positions depending on the season.

3. The Big Dipper is made of seven stars: four stars make up the "bowl" and three stars form a bent "handle."

4. If you find the Big Dipper, you can also find the Great Bear—the "handle" is the bear's tail.

BIG DIPPER

URSA MAJOR, OR "GREAT BEAR"

Where the Stars Are

There are 88 different named constellations in the night sky. Which constellations you can see changes depending on where you live on Earth and the time of year. This is because, as the Earth rotates, what you see in the sky changes.

NOW YOU KNOW!

Now you know how to find the Big Dipper. If you live in the Northern Hemisphere, you should be able to spot it all night long. (If you live in the Southern Hemisphere, get up early in the morning to see it.)

FINDING TRUE NORTH

The North Star (Polaris) can help you navigate in the dark if you're ever lost or without your compass. It will guide you to true north.

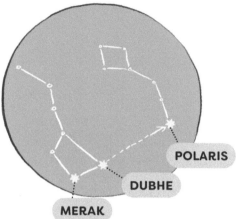

POLARIS

DUBHE

MERAK

1. Look for the Big Dipper (see page 50).

2. Now find the two stars on the side of the Big Dipper where liquid would pour out of its "bowl." These are Merak and Dubhe, called the pointer stars because they point to Polaris.

3. Imagine a line stretching through the pointer stars.

4. The pointer stars point the direction to Polaris, which is the end of the Little Dipper's handle. The Little Dipper is another group of stars that's the same shape as the Big Dipper, but smaller. It's also called Ursa Minor, or Little Bear.

5. Polaris remains fixed (meaning it doesn't move) above the North Pole—true north.

Before the Compass

Before the compass was invented, people had to use the stars to figure out which way they were going. Polaris was a very important star for all travelers.

NOW YOU KNOW!

Now you know how to find true north. Now that you can identify Polaris, research other stars and their locations.

CONNECT THE STARS

Connect the dots around Ursa Major and Ursa Minor!

Now you know how to find true north, find constellations, tell time with the sun, and predict the weather. You've earned your sky-gazing superstar badge! **Color the badge!**

CHAPTER FIVE

RESCUE RANGER

An Outdoor Adventurer has to be ready for anything. You'll need to know what to do if you get lost, how to stay found, and how to survive a night in the wilderness. Once you complete these skills, then you can teach them to your family and friends.

In this chapter, you'll learn the following skills:

- ☐ **What to do if you are lost**
- ☐ **How to use a signal mirror**
- ☐ **How to use a shelter to stay warm and dry**
- ☐ **How to find safe drinking water**
- ☐ **How to make a finding flag**

STAYING FOUND

Even Outdoor Adventurers can lose their way in the wild. In case you're ever lost, it's helpful to know how to get help and be found. Practice this activity with a group and teach this skill to anyone you know—even adults.

1. Stop. Once you realize that you are lost, stop where you are. Make sure it's a safe place.

2. Sit down. Build yourself a little nest around where you are sitting. You can use anything that you can reach from your sitting spot—rocks, sticks, or dried leaves. This is your safe zone.

3. Get your whistle out of your backpack and blow it in 3 short bursts: 1-2-3! Stop, count to 10, then blow it again. Call out in a loud voice and make lots of noise so that people can find you.

Time to Use It

Thanks to your "Bare Necessities" checklist (page xiii), you'll always have a whistle ready to blow. Your whistle is a special tool just for emergencies. Only blow it when you're lost so that you can be found. Keep it safe and quiet until you need it.

MIRROR, MIRROR

Sunlight reflected in a signal mirror can be seen up to 7 miles away. Using just the sun's rays and a small mirror, it's possible to signal for help—and here's how.

1. Point the mirror toward the sun so that it reflects light onto a nearby tree (or even your hand).

2. Slowly raise the mirror up to your eye to look through the "sighting" hole in the middle of the mirror. Make sure nothing is in the way.

3. Tilt the mirror toward the sun until you see a small, bright light. This is called the "fireball."

4. Very slowly, turn and tilt the mirror into the air so that the "fireball" can be seen by rescuers.

5. If there are no rescuers in the air, sweep the mirror along the horizon, where the earth meets the sky.

Time to Use It

Thanks to your "Bare Necessities" checklist (page xiii), you'll always have a signal mirror ready. Your signal mirror is a special tool just for emergencies. Only use it when you're lost so that you can be found.

SHELTER IN THE WILD

In Chapter 1, you learned how to build a shelter at the campsite. But you can use this skill in the wild, too, to help you stay warm and dry. It's time to put this important skill to use.

1. Find a clearing where you can build your shelter.

2. Look around and gather materials. What's close by that you can use? Do you see any leaves or branches on the ground? You can even use the poncho or emergency blanket from your "Bare Necessities" pack (page xiii).

3. Now, build your shelter. You can build the lean-to from page 5, or experiment with other structures. For example, you can tie a branch between two trees and then lean other branches against it.

4. Use loose leaves, moss, or twigs to fill in any holes in your shelter. You can also try tying your blanket or poncho above your shelter to make a rain fly. This will protect you from sun and rain.

5. Enter your shelter and try it out to make sure it is strong and safe.

Safety First

While a cave or a large hole may look like an easy shelter, these places could already be an animal's home—and they don't like surprise guests. Always build your own shelter, when you can.

WATER WARRIOR

Water is incredibly important; staying hydrated keeps us healthy and safe. Most kids need to drink about 5 cups of water each day. This activity will help you find the best places for safe, fresh water.

1. Most campgrounds have **potable** water. "Potable" means the water is safe to drink. Whenever you see potable water, be sure to fill up your water bottle.

2. In the morning, you can find water (dew) on the surface of large leaves or plants. This water is fresh and safe to drink. You can use your bandana to collect morning dew. Tie the bandana around your ankle and walk through wet grass. The bandana will absorb the water. Squeeze the fresh water into a cup, bottle, or right into your mouth.

3. Make a bandana filter. You'll need to filter water you find in the wilderness before drinking it (which means removing particles that can make you sick). For this method, you need your water bottle and an extra water container. Fold a bandana three times over the top of your empty water bottle. Slowly pour water through the bandana so that it acts like a filter. **This doesn't filter out everything, however, so it's not the safest method and should only be used if you don't have a water filter.**

Safety First

When you're looking for water, it can be tempting to drink any drops that you find. But some water sources are not safe. Rivers and streams have fast-moving water (and you don't want to be pulled in) and still water can be dirty, especially if it smells funny. It's always best to use an official water filter if you have it.

MAKE A FINDING FLAG

A finding flag is a special flag that you can tie onto your backpack so that everyone knows the backpack is yours. It can also be used to signal for help in case of emergencies. Bring items from home so that you can make your own bright flag at the campsite.

WHAT YOU'LL NEED:

☐ Found objects at campsite or from home

☐ Bandanas (use bright colors and unusual patterns)

☐ Duct tape (more colors are fun, too)

☐ Permanent markers or stickers

1. Find some fun materials from around your campsite to decorate your flag, like fallen flowers and leaves. You can also bring ribbons and buttons from home if you like.

2. Stick the items you found onto your bandana with the duct tape. Make a fun, crazy pattern or use the duct tape, markers, or stickers to spell out your initials. This will help others know that the flag is yours.

3. Tie the flag to your backpack so that everyone can see it.

Time to Use It

A finding flag isn't just fun to make; it's another tool you can use to help you stay found. People can be hard to see in a forest or from a distance. With your colorful finding flag, you can stand out and signal if you're ever lost or need help.

NOW YOU KNOW!

Now you know how to make your own finding flag. Wave this flag when you need to get someone's attention even though you are far away. Bright colors will help others to see you better. Just one more skill to learn—and it's especially fun!

SING A SILLY SONG

Wow, Outdoor Adventurer! You've learned so many skills that can help you if you ever get lost. But not everyone will always be as brave as you. Sometimes other people, like a little brother or sister, can get scared, even when there's nothing scary. This is when it helps to sing a silly song. Make your own silly songs below by filling in the missing words.

To the tune of "The Bear Went Over the Mountain"

The _____ went over the _____ (Sing 3 times)
         noun   **noun**

To see what _____ could see.
              pronoun

And all that _____ could see (Sing 2 times)
               pronoun

Was the other _____ of the _____
                 noun   **noun**

The other _____ of the _____ (Sing 2 times)
            noun   **noun**

Was all that _____ could see!
               pronoun

Example:

The girl went over the hilltop,

The girl went over the hilltop,

The girl went over the hilltop,

To see what she could see.

And all that she could see,

And all that she could see,

Was the other part of the city,

The other part of the city,

The other part of the city,

Was all that she could see!

Now you know how to be brave for others, and for yourself. If you ever get lost, you know how to keep yourself safe and signal for help. You've earned your final badge, the rescue ranger badge. **Color the badge!**

BREAKING CAMP

Before you pack up your tent and head home, here are some things you can do to keep the wilderness wild and clean for others, too.

Everyone Poops!

Everyone poops. . . . even when they're camping. Pooping can be messy and gross, but it's important to do it right. If you're in the backcountry or if there is no toilet available, you have two options:

1. Dig a "cathole" using a trowel (a small shovel). This is a hole in the ground that is at least 6 inches deep and is far away from the campsite or any water. You can poop in the hole and then bury it.

2. Pack it out. Bring a plastic bag to scoop your poop up so that you can throw it away in a trash can. If you use toilet paper, pack that out too.

No matter what you do, wash your hands with soap and water or use hand sanitizer to keep everyone safe and healthy. Keep your own toilet paper and hand sanitizer in your backpack so that you'll never be without them.

LEAVE NO TRACE

The best way to be a steward of the outdoors is to respect nature. When you leave, your campsite should look as though you were never there.

☐ Pick up all trash, even the teeny-tiny bits. If there was trash when you got there, be a great Outdoor Adventurer and pick that up, too. **Pack it out** (take it with you) to dispose of at home.

☐ Be sure any campfire is completely out and cold to the touch. If the fire pit feels hot or even warm, dump water on it so that it is cold and drowned.

☐ If you built any structures while camping, please take them down. This gives other kids the chance to practice their skills and become Outdoor Adventurers, too.

☐ Walk every corner of your campsite to make sure that nothing is left behind. It's easy to forget a tent stake, a walking stick, or even a sock.

☐ Leave any natural items in nature. This means flowers, rocks, and even sticks. When they stay where you found them, then others get to enjoy them, too.

☐ Ask your family to take lots of pictures so that you can remember your fun trip.

CONGRATULATIONS!

You are an official Outdoor Adventurer. You should be proud of all the skills you learned and the badges you completed. Don't forget to sign your Outdoors Oath (page xii) as a good caretaker of the planet.

Remember that some kids (and adults) haven't learned many of these important skills yet. The best way to teach someone is by example, so be sure to show everyone what a responsible Outdoor Adventurer you are. **Happy camping!**

RESOURCES FOR PARENTS

If you're looking to expand your child's outdoor interests and knowledge, in addition to the amazing books and resources below, pick up some of the local field guides, nature encyclopedias, and animal field guides published by DK and National Geographic Kids, available online at Amazon.com.

✎ Bear Grylls

BearGrylls.com

We really love Bear Grylls's fiction adventure books, as well as his survival and activity books. They are great to read aloud to kids, and the survival books are packed full of information (for kids ages seven and up).

✎ Earth Rangers Podcast

EarthRangers.com/podcast

Earth Rangers is a children's conservation organization that encourages kids to take action and protect biodiversity. The podcast highlights different animals and teaches kids what they can do to help. Their Earth Ranger Club also has fun missions that kids can complete to get involved.

Exploring Nature with Children

RaisingLittleShoots.com/buy-exploring-nature
-with-children

This year-long curriculum guides kids through 48 weeks
of studying nature, with seasonally themed nature walks
and activities.

Forest School Adventure: Outdoor Skills and Play for Children

by Naomi Walmsley and Dan Westall

This book is full of great ideas for getting outside and
learning about nature. It includes sections on bushcraft,
wild food, nature awareness, and games.

4-H

4-H.org

The country's largest youth development organization is
an affordable way for kids ages eight and older to learn
about the outdoors. Check online for an active chapter in
your community.

Hatchet Adventure Series

by Gary Paulsen

Gary Paulsen's fictional adventure stories, which begin with the novel *Hatchet*, are books every kid should read. While better suited for kids ages eleven and up (due to some graphic hunting scenes), the bulk of the series is focused on a kid surviving in the wild. The books captivate my outdoor-loving kids and are ones they read over and over.

Junior Ranger Programs

NPS.gov/kids/junior-rangers.htm

Every National Park hosts free Junior Ranger programs, which include activity books for each park and a swearing in as a Junior Ranger.

PBS Kids

PBSKids.org

The PBS Kids shows *Wild Kratts* and *Molly of Denali* both teach great outdoors lessons. These are shows that parents can feel good about sharing with their kids.

Tales of a Mountain Mama

TalesOfAMountainMama.com

Amelia Mayer and her team of outdoor families are always putting out new content to get families outside. Check out the sections on outdoor education and gear reviews to keep everyone feeling comfortable.

Think Outside

ThinkOutsideBoxes.com

This monthly subscription box is fantastic for providing hands-on education to help kids ages four to fourteen learn about the outdoors. It is hands-down our favorite and is worth every penny.

Wild Math

WildMathCurriculum.com

Wild Math is an awesome curriculum for kids (grades K through 5) that encourages an exploration of math in the wild. It's simple, affordable, and a fun way to get outside.

ABOUT THE AUTHOR

Amelia Mayer lives with her husband, their five children, and their dog in Grand Teton National Park. She finds her sanity outdoors where the fresh air seems to dull any whining and relieve any stress. This is where her family bonds best and where their best memories are made together.

She has a passion for getting families active and outdoors, despite that sometimes being a very hard thing. Amelia loves to hike, bike, camp, cross-country and downhill ski, and explore the mountains of Wyoming. And she (usually) prefers to do those activities with her family.

Amelia works to educate and inspire, sharing her rough moments (everyone has them!) online via social media. You can find her outdoor community at TalesOfAMountainMama.com, and on Instagram, Facebook, and Pinterest @MtnMamaTales.

CPSIA information can be obtained
at www.ICGtesting.com
Printed in the USA
JSHW011212240322
24012JS00003B/11

9 781648 762093